Accelerated Learning

Advanced Learning Strategies to
Learn Faster, Remember More
and be More Productive

By Patrick Lightman

Table of Contents

Introduction

I want to thank you and congratulate you for downloading the book, *"Accelerated Learning"*.

This book contains proven steps and strategies on how to enhance your learning so you can acquire knowledge at a much faster rate.

For many people, learning in general is not easy. Many people often struggle with mastering the most basic of concepts when trying to learn something new, and muddle through school year after year with mediocre grades, and by the time they should be thinking about entering college and getting an advanced education, many have either given up or they don't care.

It doesn't help that parents, teachers, and administrators in schools buy into the old-fashioned idea cookie cutter education thus creating an endless cycle of students who are barely getting by. Fast forward all of that into a mediocre career where schools have produced class after class of students who have just lost the will to even try to learn any more.

For years, we have seen generation after generation of students lose interest in study and sad to say, it only results in a lack of interest in life in general. We are amazing creatures that have been designed to learn but when you have been mentally boxed into learning in only one approved way, one that goes against your natural grain of absorbing information, it can be very easy to give up and lose interest.

Your motivation will wane and unfortunately it will affect your interest in continuing to learn in later years and by extension have a major impact on your quality of life.

However, because we have been designed to be lifelong learners, it is more important than ever that we do more when we study than just absorb information, we must also find a way to enjoy it. We live in an age where our knowledge base is constantly changing and we have to be prepared to master new things at every stage of life. It doesn't matter if you're school-aged or a senior citizen, the need to learn is directly connected to how well you can navigate the world around you and all you have to do in it.

In our modern age, new information is being released at phenomenal rates. Those who are not comfortable with not only lifelong learning but the ability to consume the information quickly will soon be left behind. This makes it more important than ever for us to embrace this new knowledge and develop a strategy that will allow us to always remain ahead of the game no matter what information is in front of us.

In the following pages of this book, we will teach you the fundamentals of accelerated learning and how to apply it in your daily lives. Together, we will learn:

- What is accelerated learning
- What you must do before you start to learn

- Basic strategies you can add to your existing study plan

- Why memory plays such an important role in learning

- How to take a negative learning experience and turn it into a positive

- And more

If you're serious about mastering new learning strategies and how you can change your world through accelerated learning, it's time to turn the page and join us on a whole new journey of learning in a whole new way. Thanks again for downloading this book, I hope you enjoy it!

The information provided herein is stated to be truthful and consistent, in that any liability, in terms of inattention or otherwise, by any usage or abuse of any policies, processes, or directions contained within is the solitary and utter responsibility of the recipient reader. Under no circumstances will any legal responsibility or blame be held against the publisher for any reparation, damages, or monetary loss due to the information herein, either directly or indirectly.

Respective authors own all copyrights not held by the publisher.

The information herein is offered for informational purposes solely and is universal as so. The presentation of the information is without contract or any type of guarantee assurance.

The trademarks that are used are without any consent, and the publication of the trademark is without permission or backing by the trademark owner. All trademarks and brands within this book are for clarifying purposes only and are owned by the owners themselves, not affiliated with this document.

Chapter 1: What is Accelerated Learning

We all need to be lifelong learners. It is key to our having a productive life and getting all the things we need to make our lives complete. Accelerated Learning is a program that basically reframes the way you've viewed learning all along. Many people are of the belief that learning is a rote exercise that involves the memorizing of long lists of facts and figures so that they can pass a test or obtain a good score however, accelerated learning is much more than that. It is a strategy that will help you to break out of that traditional line of thought opening your mind up to an endless parade of possibilities.

Once you come to a clearer understanding of what accelerated learning really is, you will be better able to set-up a more efficient environment around you, one that is more conducive to learning. You will be more effective in choosing the conditions under which you learn, one that will make it easier for your mind to absorb more information and be where you can take the new knowledge that you have acquired and extend it in practical ways that can apply to all sorts of situations in your life. In essence, accelerated learning will make you more adept at getting your brain to receive information and retain it, recalling it whenever needed in ways that will best benefit your life.

There are several fundamentals of accelerated learning that make all of this possible.

It is a means of boosting your learning power - each of us has his own way of acquiring information. When you know how to tap into your own personal learning style, learning will feel more natural to you, making it easier to acquire new knowledge, and by extension you will be able to absorb it much faster.

You will be able to tap into your five senses, which is the body's natural way of absorbing information. When you learn how to enhance your visual, auditory, and kinesthetic abilities, the information you take in will become a natural extension of yourself and the new knowledge will become more like second nature to you.

To accomplish this, there is a six-stage process to accelerated learning that has proven to be very effective. The six stages can be best remembered with the acronym M-A-S-T-E-R, which stands for:

- **M**ind set to positive:
- **A**cquire the knowledge
- **S**earch out the meaning
- **T**rigger your memory
- **E**xhibit what you know
- **R**eflect on your learning

With this type of program, the learning relies more on the doing, practicing, and applying the new knowledge rather than just reading, hearing, or seeing things. When you apply these types of techniques, you begin to enjoy your learning much more than you would otherwise.

Basically, accelerated learning is the study of how **your mind works.** Not just the study of the mind in general but because each of our minds works differently, you need to understand the mechanics of your own mind.

When you examine the brain itself, you will find amazing features that will boggle your imagination and stimulate your thinking. You may not be aware of the fact that your brain contains as many as 100 billion brain cells (or neurons) but this is not what makes your ability to learn so impressive. It is the 20,000 or so connections that are branching off from each of those neurons that make learning possible.

You don't have to be a math major in order to see the benefits of these features. Each time one of those trillions of dendrites light up, a thought occurs, a memory is formed, knowledge is acquired, and experiences are developed. Today, with all of our modern technology, scientists are actually able to see these thoughts as they occur in the brain helping us to come to a much clearer understanding of how learning happens and what works best for each of us. This understanding of how our brain works and the best way to tap into it makes up the crux of what we call accelerated learning.

Our Brain Stem

We can start by understanding the basic physiology of the brain itself. Our brain stem, the part of the brain that sits at the base of the skull and connects to the spinal column is primarily responsible for our basic life functions, those actions that we do without thinking. It controls and regulates our heart beat, our breathing, and our basic instincts. At first glance, you may not think this has anything to do with how you learn, however, once you realize that this same region of the brain is also the instinctual center of the body, you will start to see why it is so key to how we react to our external environment.

A good example of this is the instinctual flight or fight response that we all have. Think of how well you learn if you're feeling threatened or angry. When these negative emotions appear your mind literally shuts down and your only thought is to restore your consciousness to safety. When the mind senses negativity, our learning process begins to shut down but when our minds are in a more positive condition, we are more receptive to what we experience in our immediate environment and we are in a better position to receive new knowledge and retain it.

Understanding this is one of the key elements of accelerated learning. It helps us to understand just how our emotional state of mind impacts our learning. At this point, you have already learned one of the keys to mastering accelerated learning. Controlling our emotional state and making sure that we are in a positive frame of mind can automatically speed up the learning process.

Our Limbic System

Our limbic system is the part of the brain that is literally wrapped around the brain stem like a collar. There are two key components here are the hypothalamus and the amygdala. This part also plays a significant role in controlling your emotions. While the brain stem focuses on controlling instinctual emotions related to protecting your survival, the limbic system controls emotions related to your personal feelings, working constantly to keep a healthy balance within the body.

It also is responsible for the release of hormones, let's you know when you're thirsty, manages your metabolism, immune system, and your **long-term memory** (an important element in the learning process).

Your hypothalamus and amygdala are key components in managing your emotions and developing your own goal-seeking behavior. This helps us to understand why we are more inclined to respond to emotional experiences better than just plain old logical reasoning. The very fact that the same part of the brain that regulates emotions also controls our memory and since learning is completely ineffective if you can't recall it, the two must work in tandem. One without the other is fruitless. So, when you realize that the same part of the brain controls both areas you can easily see why you need to focus on them together to speed up the learning process.

If you were asked to remember your best teacher in school, chances are you can conjure up visions of one immediately. You recall what they taught you, how you felt during the lesson, and liked every detail of your time with them. Other teachers may have left vague impressions that you might struggle to recall. You remember your favorite teachers because of your positive emotional experiences you had with them. Teachers that did not connect with you on such a primal level have been easily forgotten, their names lost somewhere in the many folds of your mind.

According to many researchers, when the brain is in a positive emotional state, it releases pleasure chemicals called endorphins, which then trigger a release of a neurotransmitter called acetylcholine that literally works as a "lubricant" basically greasing the connections made between the neurons in the brain, allowing it to process new information more efficiently. This is why emotionally stimulating lessons like art, drama, music, and others are often very successful as a means of teaching new information.

The same is not true of those who experience negative emotions while studying. According to researchers reporting in the journal *Scientific American*, the limbic system acts like a switchboard connecting our senses to the brain's cortex. It analyzes each piece of new information coming in and decides whether or not it should be connected to the cortex or not. If the new information is deemed to be stressful (negative in nature) it could literally be transferred to the more primitive areas of the brain (the brain stem) where it can trigger more instinctual behavior rather than up to the cortex or the "thinking" part of the brain.

This is also the reason why before any learning period, it is important to use relaxation exercises in an attempt to reduce any negative emotions you might be experiencing before a study session.

The Neocortex

Located above the limbic brain is the neocortex. This is the very heart of your intelligence, the part of the brain that allows humans to think and process information in a way that no other creature on the planet can do. This is where your mind makes decisions, organizes your view of the world and stores any experiences you may have had. It is also the place where memory and speech are produced, where your appreciation of the arts lies, and where much of the learning happens.

The neocortex can be divided into different parts (referred to as lobes). There is a lobe dedicated to every aspect the brain must process; speech, hearing, vision, touch, taste. As we use each of our five senses, we store the memories of the data into different areas of the neocortex. If you hope to develop strong attachments to the new information you learn, it is imperative that you engage your emotional core in the process. This natural physiology of the brain is evidence that engaging your senses while learning is an important element that ensures that you can remember whatever it is you decide to learn.

Your Two Hemispheres

As you become more familiar with the three different parts of the brain, you'll also notice that the brain has two very distinct sides called the right and left hemispheres. Each of these hemispheres is responsible for different functions in the body. While both sides are connected by the corpus callous (a network consisting of approximately 300 million neurons) working as a shuttle moving information back and forth between the two hemispheres, research has shown that each side of the brain is primarily responsible for different things.

The left brain is considered to be the area where our logical thinking takes place. It is responsible for all things academic; computing mathematical processes, analyzing data and situations, sequencing information, and developing reasoning. The right brain is the more creative side of your thinking. It is where you develop your sense of rhythm, appreciation for music, visual impressions, images, color, etc. This is the part of the brain that is constantly searching for patterns, and analogies in the world around you and where you develop conceptual thoughts in relation to more abstract ideas like love, beauty, and loyalty.

While each side of the brain is primarily responsible for very specific roles, both of them are involved in the process of learning. A perfect example of this can be seen in how the brain processes a simple movement. Let's say that you are watching a red ball as it rolls along a flat surface. Your brain needs to fire up several areas of the brain in order to process what is happening. It processes the color and shape in one area, movement in another area, location in another area. In fact, four different areas of the brain must be activated for you to understand what is happening right in front of your eyes.

Yes, each hemisphere is dominant in certain elements but they are both needed to learn something well. However, if you are a person that is more left brain then your style of learning will favor the logical, more linear type of learning. You will want to be given step-by-step instructions of each part of the process but a right brain learner will want to see a more global image of the subject matter.

It is not that you only use one side of the brain or another but rather, it is finding ways of learning that appeals to your more dominant side of your brain. While both sides are active participants in the learning process, discovering which side is your dominant side and tailoring your lessons to that side will allow you to absorb information much faster than ever before.

It is a whole brain endeavor. This is why music has proven to be such a powerful way to teach lessons.

When you listen to a popular song, your left brain focuses on the lyrics while the right brain is processing the melody. The limbic system is engaged in the deeper meaning of the words and tapping into your emotions. Very quickly, you will know the song and remember. Years later, you will hear just a few bars and your mind will trigger every note as if you had just heard it for the first time. This is because it engages the "whole brain" in the process. This is the core principle behind accelerated learning; it is a means of stretching your mind by engaging all facets of the brain in the learning process.

Our brains are powerful instruments and we are just now beginning to learn how to make good use of it. Most of us enjoy those activities that engage the whole brain in the thinking process because we are tapping into our emotions, our logical and reasoning abilities, as well as our creative side. We tend to lose interest however, when we are given exercises that only engage a single part of our brain. Exercises that require the memorization of long lists of information, an endless series of mathematical problems to calculate, or any type of repetitive work tends to shut down parts of our brain causing us to lose emotional attachment to the material.

The Magic Eight

Now that you understand the importance of engaging the whole brain in the learning process, it's time for you to kick your learning up another notch. The Magic Eight refers to a new way of measuring intelligence. The Theory of Multiple

Intelligence, developed by Harvard Professor Howard Gardner measures not how smart you may be based on an IQ test but rather determines how you use the intelligence you have.

His thoughts are that intelligence varies depending on the circumstances at the time and our ability to navigate them. All human beings have a unique body of skills that we rely on during varying times in our lives. We tap into those skills when we need them in ways that are unique to each of us. So, if you were stranded in the Australian outback the skills you need would be very different from those needed on the streets of New York City. Your ability to survive in each of those situations would depend on a completely different set of knowledge that you would have at your disposal.

Our intelligence therefore is our ability to manage a wide variety of problems that can range from something as basic as deciding what to wear to something that is as complicated as getting out of life or death situations. According to Gardner there are at least nine different types of intelligences we can tap into to resolve those problems. While we all have some level of each one in our repertoire, we each have several more dominant intelligences that we favor when we are trying to acquire new knowledge.

Linguistic: Linguistic Intelligence is your ability to communicate with words. You can absorb information through reading, writing, or verbally.

Logical-Mathematical: your ability to calculate figures, reason on things, or to mentally process things in a logical and systematic manner.

Visual-Spatial: Your ability to process images, visualize things in your mind's eye, and imagine future results.

Musical: your ability to create music, to compose, sing, or understand musical pieces. It also includes your ability to maintain a certain rhythm.

Bodily-Kinesthetic: your ability to use your body in variety of ways. This could involve using your hands to create products, to physically demonstrate how something is done, to present ideas in a physical manner, to express your emotions through body language.

Interpersonal: your ability to work with and interact well with others. You can relate well with others, show empathy, and understanding, and recognize other people's motivations and aspirations.

Intrapersonal: The ability to self-analyze and reflect on past experiences. To be able to sit back and analyze your past behaviors, personal feelings, and set goals based on them.

Naturalist: your ability to tap into nature and make distinctions in the natural world. To be able to identify flora and fauna in your environment and understand the basic sciences of biology.

Existential: your ability to tap into the deeper meaning of life and to connect to a higher form of existence.

The ability to recognize the spiritual being that lies underneath the physical and mental person.

In traditional educational settings, the focus was always on either the linguistic or mathematical skills, which worked well for some students but for those students who weren't strong in these areas, where their natural intelligence fell into one of the other categories, they often fell through the cracks. Learning was not an emotionally stimulating experience and could prove to be extremely daunting and uncomfortable.

All of these elements make up the core of accelerated learning and give you the keys to acquiring new knowledge at a faster rate than ever before. By using these tools, you learn to tap into your own unique combination of intelligences and develop the techniques needed to use your whole brain in order to absorb the information much easier and retain it better. By doing this, you make it possible to learn much faster and get more enjoyment out of the entire process.

Chapter 2: Preparing to Learn

We've all been told that it is important to have a good learning environment to help us to learn but we never completely understood why. After decades of research though, we understand that our immediate external environment can have a significant impact on just how our brains absorb new information. But few of us think about how we can adapt our internal environment to enhance the experience of learning too.

The reality is clear, there are several factors and environmental conditions that have a direct impact on how well you learn. Once you understand these different elements and how they affect your learning, you'll be able to create the best conditions to make your learning experience easier and faster.

Your immediate environment is not just physical but can also be mental and emotional as well. Some of these things are within your ability to control them while others are not.

Your Attention Span

According to the nonprofit group Technology, Entertainment, and Design, (you're probably more familiar with it as TED Talks) most of us have a very limited attention span. Unless you're a rather exceptional individual, your ability to focus on a single topic is usually maxed out at approximately 18 minutes. When you are forced to listen to lectures that run into hours, you are losing a significant part of the lesson that may be valuable to you.

Of course, all of this is relative. You can focus more on a two-hour movie because it is passive activity. Your brain is not forced to conceptualize the information contained. Visualization work is already provided for you. On the other hand, when you are trying to absorb a lecture, you are expected to use much more brain power. You are expected to participate in open discussions, ask questions, etc. This can cause your brain to tire out and you will need a break as your mental fatigue begins to set in.

The reality is that you can only absorb information when your brain is focused. By scheduling study times that last longer than the brain is capable of absorbing information you'll find yourself spinning your wheels and losing valuable data. So, by scheduling shorter study times with regular breaks in between, you give your mind a chance to rest and process the information you've taken in before adding more on top of it.

When setting up your study schedule, factor in the periods when you tend to be the most active. Some of us are morning people and can perform well first things in the morning while others may be more night owls and can muster up more attention late at night. These are the optimum times for you to carve out study time allowing your brain to absorb more in a shorter period of time.

This does not mean that you have to limit your study time to precisely 18 minutes to be effective. Most people find success by using the 30-50-minute study sessions. If you choose a 50-minute session, you can have two 20-minute study periods with a 10-minute break in between. If you choose a 30-minute session you can have 15-minute session with a 5-minute break before another 10-minute session as a follow up.

Whatever you choose, make sure that it allows you to maximize study time without allowing you to slip into brain fatigue. Surprisingly enough, you'll find that if you follow this pattern you'll absorb more information, retain it better, and you'll enjoy studying much more than if you try to schedule in an hour long cram session.

Concepts Before Facts

Another important consideration is the order of the information you want to learn. In traditional school settings students are often inundated with long lists of facts without any practical application that allow them to mentally connect with the information they are given. According to one researcher, there are two different types of learning. There is the surface and the deep learning styles.

With surface learning, you are able to accumulate entire lists of facts to memorize whereas with deep learning your mind focuses on the abstract meaning of the subject and how it applies to reality. You might conclude that deep learning is more important but in reality, there is a time and place for both types of learning.

When your study is focused entirely on memorization, your brain starts to isolate single pieces of information without any way of relating them to a particular concept. There is nothing anchoring them in your mind, however, when you are given them in a context situation you can start to identify connections, patterns, and relationships between the information then your brain has something to hold onto.

The ability to identify patterns is what makes learning useful, otherwise the information you've learned has no useful purpose that makes the mind want to hold onto them. If you can find that underlying pattern (right brain activity) or concept and follow it through to a logical conclusion you would be able to determine the relatability and will make a more personal connection to it.

For example, suppose you are studying the Miranda rights in your history class. With surface learning, you would learn the names of the Supreme Court Justices, the lawyers that argued the case, and the names of all the other parties that were involved. You may even remember the exact date the case was heard, the number of votes and how many appeals it had leading up to the case.

But while all of these facts have a bearing on the subject, they don't connect you to the information you're taking in. They mean nothing to you, they are just lists of information.

However, if you wanted to look more deeply at the subject you would search out the underlying concept that surrounds the reason for this information, then when you did come across the facts relating to the case, they would be much easier to remember. So, concepts allow you to give the specific facts and details involving the subject a home base in your brain, giving you a personal connection to the case and how it relates to you and your life today. You would learn about the rights of the defendants and how they have evolved and can affect you today.

As you master this skill of concept learning you will learn how to categorize different facts by the specific attributes, identify patterns, and integrate them into your mind in a way that will help you to recall them later.

This technique can be applied to more than just school and book learning. It can be used to develop new skills all throughout life and as a result give more meaning to your life in general. It helps you to understand the main point of each new thing you learn, not just the facts surrounding it. When you are looking for new information, look for more than just "what" happened, look for the "why" as well. It is the "why" that will give you the concept behind everything you learn.

Your Frustration Level

Being an accelerated learner does not in any way imply that you will master everything right the first time. In fact, the truth is just the opposite. You will fail and fail often, especially when you are trying to master a new skill. In accelerated learning, this is referred to as "Productive Failure," a term coined by Manu Kapur, a researcher at the National Institute of Education in Singapore. His theory lies in the fact that if you give a student a reliable model to learn from, continuing guidance and support, and maintain it until they master their skill it is a key secret to success. As a result of supplying them with a safe place to test out their new theories, they will flounder again and again, learning and mastering a little more of the skill until they reach a point of full mastery.

It is the basis of all learning experiences we have as a child. When we are born, we come with a completely blank slate. We do not know how to talk, walk, play, interact, or even take care of our basic needs. However, it is through trial and error that we slowly master all of these skills and master them to the point that they become second nature to us. We learn to walk by repeatedly falling and pulling ourselves back up, we learn to speak by constantly making sounds, mimicking the sounds we hear from others around us until we actually form words.

At some point, we start to view failure as something bad and something to be ashamed of and it is at this point that we start to flounder in our learning. We lose our confidence and begin to see learning as a chore rather than a natural life experience. However, it has been shown through several research studies, that the ability to learn how to solve problems comes from those failed experiences that we are so reluctant to have. When we attempt something and fail at it, our minds have to work towards figuring out what went wrong and then trying several attempts at the problem until we get it right. By avoiding the "mistakes" we are actually restricting our ability to learn and grow.

With each failure, you learn more about the specific problem and can use that knowledge more effectively the next time you attempt to find a solution. According to Kapur, there are three different factors that make embracing failure an effective learning tool.

1. It allows you to work on problems that offer a challenge

2. It provides you with the opportunity to explain and detail the steps in your process
3. It allows you to make comparisons and contrasts for both good and bad solutions

As a result, with each attempt to solve a problem and each successive failure, you reinforce the knowledge you have, correct wrong conclusions, and refine the learning process all at the same time. Sad to say, at some point, society and educators in general have reached the conclusion that the end result is what's important and not the process it took to get there. By embracing your failures, the ability to work out problems becomes the primary concern and students are less reluctant to hide their mistakes allowing everyone to address the weak areas in learning, making it faster and more efficient.

The key here is to control your level of frustration that is often associated with failure. By viewing these mistakes as stepping stones rather than a blight on your character, you can develop a strategy that will help to solve the problem in a more productive way allowing you to learn from your experiences rather than to allow them to deflate you and diminish your self-confidence.

You must be realistic here. After repeated attempts to solve a problem, you will eventually feel frustration and at times have to fight of the temptation to quit. If you allow those feelings to overtake you, it could lead to excessive anxiety that will eventually impact your studies. But if you expect this type of frustration ahead of time, you can develop a plan to respond to it in a more positive way. More often than not, when frustration levels get high, it may be best to take a break from the problem and allow your brain a chance to recover. Focus your attention on something else for a while and when you come back to it, you'll see the problem through fresh eyes, with less anxiety associated with it. Often when you have a more relaxed frame of mind to work with, the answers flow much more easily than if you are under stress.

So, while preparing your immediate external environment to create an atmosphere that is more conducive to study, knowing how to prepare mentally for study is equally if not more important. So often, people delve into the depths of study without understanding their own psychological and emotional make-up, or even knowing how their own brain works and as a result, create an environment that could turn out to be hit or miss for the learning experience. By preparing yourself mentally, understanding your limitations, and working within the confines of your own ability, you avoid spinning your wheels in the study process and open yourself up to an unlimited potential that will accelerate your learning in many ways.

Chapter 3: Bringing Your A Game

As we have already learned, when you know how the brain works it makes it much easier to accumulate new information. There are some very specific strategies that will help you to accelerate your learning by bringing your A game to the table.

Let's go back to what we have already come to understand about the brain and how it works. We've already discussed that when you learn something new, you create a connection in one of the trillions of connections. Each new piece of knowledge you acquire is stored in a specific neuron in your brain. It arrives at that particular neuron via connections called dendrites.

Learning is the process of creating new connections for each new piece of information you pick up.

A good example of this is when you meet someone. Let's say his name is Alfred. Once you have that knowledge, there is a neuron set aside for your knowledge of Alfred. If when you meet him, you see his face, there is a dendrite connection created that plants a visual image of Alfred in your brain. If you shook his hand, you now have a textile memory of him created in a new dendrite. If you noticed his smile, listened to his voice, noticed his after shave, or even engaged in a little banter, you create a new dendrite in the brain for each piece of new information about him. The more connections you create, the easier it will be to recall this valuable information at a later time.

As you can see, it is not enough to want to learn and to be motivated, you also need to bring your many other elements into play with every bit of detail you hope to learn.

One of the most unfortunate things about traditional learning is that it is often presented too much by rote. The idea of teachers spewing out information in a singular fashion and students being expected to parrot it back to them in a certain order has removed much of the imagination from the entire experience.

To accomplish this, you must be willing to go beyond the books and the calculators to enhance your learning. One would be purely amazed at the power a few simple exercises can have "before" the learning begins. Once applied and put to the test, your whole body will be prepared to engage in learning without hesitation and in fact, will be looking forward to it with a great deal of anticipation.

All of this starts with just a little creative thinking. It starts with the ability to visualize your success at tackling the more difficult subjects before you begin to study. This will frame your mind in such a way that it will boost your motivation and confidence in the subject you are about to undertake. Already, around the globe, this is a practice that has been put in place with many world-class athletes. But this skill does not have to be limited to those in the athletic arena. Whether you're doing scientific research, preparing for a business meeting, or you're just looking for a solid political standing, your ability to envision the end goal before you start will be extremely successful in mentally preparing you for the lessons you hope to master.

This brings us to one key element when it comes to learning. It requires some personal reflection about the act of learning itself. Motivation - or the belief that you really do want to learn can make a huge difference in bringing your "A Game" to the experience. When you are not motivated, commitment to follow through on the lessons is often weak, if not non-existent. A lack of motivation or a desire to master the topic you're trying to absorb could close your mind off from any type of learning experience.

To determine your personal level of motivation, you need to do a little personal introspection. Whether you're trying to master a new skill, tackle a new subject, or just improve your already existing knowledge, your personal investment in the task will weigh heavily on whether or not you will succeed. If you are reluctant, have developed a negative attitude about it, or are in any way unreceptive to the lesson, you are more inclined to view it as a burdensome chore and inevitably setting yourself up for failure.

This does not mean that you won't have some negative feelings. Any time you tackle anything new, doubts, fears, and anxieties are just a natural part of it. After all, you're about to embark on a whole new territory where you will most likely start out navigating unfamiliar terrain, but your level of motivation is the single most important key to helping you to overcome them.

You will have to make an active choice to push aside those negative feelings and change them for more positive viewpoints. Remember, the more actively engaged in the process you are the better you'll be able to learn. This is a factor that you can control.

Know Your Why

No matter what new endeavor you hope to undertake, it is more important than ever that you understand why you are doing it. This is just as important when it comes to learning. Ask yourself, what you hope to gain from learning this new information. You have to visualize a positive end result in order to be successful and get started on the right track.

There are probably many reasons why you may have chosen to take on the subject you're trying to master. Perhaps you want to get a promotion on your job, maybe you're looking to master a new skill or talent, or you need to keep up a specific GPA in order to get into the university you plan to attend. Since we all study for different reasons, we will have very different reasons for wanting to learn something new. Just make sure that your why is something strong enough to motivate you to tackle the steps and techniques we will be learning later on in this book.

It will pay off in a big way if you take the time to ask realistic questions and search out your reason for tackling your particular topic. And don't be embarrassed by your answers, it can be quite cathartic to honestly appraise your inner motivations in helping you to achieve your goals. So, if you're truly not interested in studying Quantum Physics in your university class and the only reason you signed up was because of that cute guy in the front row, it helps to understand that from the very beginning.

Whatever the reason, your motivation has to be strong enough to boost your desire to learn. This means that you must search out the benefits you will gain and be able to visualize yourself achieving them before you start. This requires a strong sense of imagination as you do this. Our imagination is an extremely powerful weapon and being able to harness it and use it to move us to advance towards our goals could be the most valuable weapon you have in your arsenal.

Once you've identified your "why" then you need to play a game of Mind Switch. Think of this like driving a car. You may have a good engine, fuel in the tank, oil, and everything you need to move the car where you need to go but if you're not able to put it in gear, then no matter what you want, the car is not going to move, period.

So, once you know your why, you then need to start getting your whole body prepared to engage in the learning process. Start by doing some simple breathing exercises. Take in a few deep breaths, filling your lungs with air, then take a long, slow exhale, pushing your stomach out as you do. Relax your neck and jaw muscles (this is the area of the body that tends to hold the most tension).

Finally, set the environment by playing some relaxing music, something that will help to put you into the right frame of mind. We've already learned that the brain is an incredible learning machine but it can only function well when it is in a relaxed state. As soon as you begin to introduce stress into the equation, it is almost as if you've wiped your mind clean. Before you attempt to study anything on your subject, it is very important that you make sure that you are in a relaxed state mentally.

To mentally relax before your lesson, try doing a few visualization exercises. It is one thing to have a goal that you are working for and it is another thing entirely to **believe** that you will master that goal. This is where visualization comes in. Take the time to see your success in mastering your subject in your mind's eye. This is much easier if you know how to engage all of your senses in this exercise.

1. See yourself completing your lesson and mastering the task you are trying to learn
2. Feel the sense of satisfaction and pride in knowing that you have accomplished your goal
3. Hear the comments of praise and recognition you will receive from other people

The more you are able to engage the senses, the easier it will be for you to see your success before you ever start your first lesson. This method of mental preparation works as a cocoon that will insulate you from external negativity in your environment. The more relaxed you are the easier it will be to shut out the craziness and chaos in the world around you so you can concentrate more on your lessons.

This works even better if you are able to find a place where you can shut the world out and completely isolate yourself from all things external. If you have a quiet place to create your own physical environment you will do much better. There you can create a pleasing visual atmosphere, add in the kind of music that is soothing to your soul, and even enhance it with essential oils, giving you the kind of fragrances that you enjoy. Adding a few plants, artwork, or just letting the natural sunlight stream in can do wonders for mentally getting you ready to study.

Becoming successful when it comes to study is really a mental game. Your mind is an interesting anomaly. You need to use brain power to learn but just like any other tool, you need to know how to use it to your advantage in order to get the best out of it. One way to do this is through positive affirmations.

By repeating out loud positive things about yourself, eventually your mind will begin to believe that your goals are possible and will start working to help you achieve them. For example, making the expression "I am confident about learning" even when you believe internally that the task is huge, will build up the motivation you need to succeed. The key here is to make sure that your expressions are positive enough. For example, rather than making statements like..."I wish I were more confident" try saying "I feel confident and sure that I can accomplish this task." Simply make the statement as if it were already true and eventually, the mind will accept it and give you exactly what you need to succeed.

Don't try to over complicate this step. In fact, it works best if you keep your affirmations positive and simple. They are far easier to remember and are more likely to be successful. Don't be shy about doing this. Some people feel as if they must appear crazy to others. Imagine the looks you get if you are walking down the street, talking to yourself before a class or before your study session. Still, try to avoid this type of thinking. After all, most of us are exposed to negative comments for the better part of our lives, if we balance the scales with a few positive ones, we are much more likely to succeed and become a successful learner than if we let the negativity from others enter into our world.

Make it a habit to repeat your affirmations whenever possible and even more often when you are faced with a particular challenge during your studies. As you say them, try to bring in visualization by imagining yourself actually accomplishing your goals and benefiting from them.

Your Goals

One very important element to successful learning is that you need to know exactly what you're aiming for. You already know that you want to master a specific task or achieve a certain goal but if that is all you do, it will be difficult to find success. When you are setting your goals for each session, you need to delve a little deeper into what you want to accomplish.

This is where you want to refine your goals and **create a plan of action** that will help you to get there. It is not enough for you to set out to cover a set number of pages during each study session. While that may be a target you want to reach it does not feed into your goals successfully. To be successful, you need to have a clear view of what your study session hopes to achieve and believe that you can successfully achieve it.

According to a study of several peak performers and successful people, it revealed that they all had an above-average ability to use their imagination and visualization to create a plan of action. In fact, they all had one specific thing in common. They started every task with a very clear picture of what they wanted to accomplish at the end.

This type of imagery involves not just conjuring up pictures of success in your mind but will require you to engage all of your senses. When you are creating your end goal, you should not only see the images you want but also hear the sounds, feel the sensations, and even smell or taste the elements in your picture. Needless to say, this is a very deep and profound type of imagery that once mastered, can prove to be one of the most effective learning tools in your arsenal.

This technique works because as impressive as the brain can be, it does not have the ability to distinguish between an actual event and one that has been created. It will use the same electrochemical pathways to process both. So, if you can create a positive enough visual image of your goal, your brain will believe it and will accept it as real, making it possible for you to accomplish your goals.

A perfect example of this can be easily illustrated with an exercise. Imagine you are in your home and you are about to make lemonade. You have chosen several large but firm lemons. In your mind, pick one up and feel its dimpled surface. It is firm and slightly heavy for its small size.

Raise the lemon to your nose and inhale its strong scent of citrus.

Now, with a sharp knife, cut the lemon in half. As the knife slices through it, notice the light spray of juice as a few tiny drops break free from the skin and permeates the air. The inner skin is in direct contrast with the pale yellow color of the juice as it gently flows out. Now, the smell is a little stronger than before.

Raise one half of the lemon to your mouth and take a big bite, letting the juices bathe the inside of your mouth before swallowing. Taste the sourness of it.

As you perform this type of imagery, notice what is happening in real life. Chances are your mouth is watering a little as you taste the sourness of the lemon. Maybe you squinted up your lips and you might have even winced a little as you thought about how it tastes. But none of this is actually real yet your body responded just the same.

What you have experienced is something we call synesthesia. In your mind, you created the feel, the sight, the smell, and the taste and your brain responded to it as if you were really doing these things. It triggered the salivary glands in your mouth and told them to cleanse your palate of the sour taste. Even reading this book (or any other book) is a form of synesthesia. The words are not real but they are designed to lead you to create an image in your mind, which directly controls what your actions will be.

By applying this type of imagery to your studies, it send s powerful message to your subconscious that tells you that what you are reading, imagining, or creating is actually real. Not only will this help you to develop powerful tools to accelerate your learning but it will also make learning an experience you are not likely to forget.

After putting yourself in the proper state of mind to study, you will create an atmosphere that will not only relieve much of the stress associated with study but will also give you a certain level of confidence in the belief that you can succeed in reaching your goals. This is often referred to as a "resourceful" frame of mind because it gives your brain several positive resources from which it can call upon when the study becomes challenging.

You have just given yourself the first of several key strategies to help you get ready to learn. Preparing your mind to a more positive mental state that is ready to learn. The next chapter will give you five more techniques that will help you to succeed as an accelerated learner. They are simple, free, and practical to use and are in a form that no other person could rob you of. We may not have the power to change our external environment and what happens around us, but we do have the power to control what goes into our mind and how it influences our behavior. With these tools at our disposal, we are ready to bring our A game into the study process and in the end, we will learn in a way that we never could have before.

Chapter 4: Basic Techniques to Speed Up the Learning Process

Now that you have mentally prepared for the study, you are ready to jump into the accelerated learning techniques that will prove to be even more effective. When you read the words, *accelerated learning* you are likely thinking that it involves simply learning faster but there is much more involved than that.

Many people are of the belief that accelerated learning means you will read over material one time, remember it and use it from then on. While elements of that thought may be true, accelerated learning does not mean that you won't' have to study; it does not mean that we can simply open up your mind, pour in the knowledge and it will be stored in perpetuity. You will still have to study, you will still have to put for the effort to acquire the knowledge you are trying to achieve. However, if you apply the techniques we are about to discuss, you will learn the information with less stress and anxiety, and you will feel more satisfied with the results you achieve. You will feel confident about what you learn and you will not feel overwhelmed even when trying to master more complicated topics.

The techniques to actually apply to the learning process are the key components to helping you acquire knowledge faster and the way they are applied are the primary reason why you will be able to recall that new knowledge when you need it. There are six different techniques involved in mastering accelerated learning. We've already discussed the first one, now let's look at the other five.

Strategy #2 Acquire the Information

As we've already discussed, everyone of us has a unique composite of learning styles so the way one person will acquire new knowledge is not the way another person would. You may be primarily a kinesthetic learner where you have to learn by doing things, touching things, and actively participating in any type of exercise in order to learn where another student may simply be able to master the knowledge simply by reading the material in front of them.

It is always a good idea to sit down and figure out exactly what method of learning works best for you. Some people learn when they are left alone to figure things out while others may need the guidance of a teacher hovering over them. Some may require a perfectly tidy work area where someone else may need a little chaos.

Whatever your preferences, when you are ready to acquire knowledge there is one thing that you will need to keep in mind. Your learning experience **must be active** and not passive. The more you are engaged in the activity of acquiring knowledge the easier ti will be to absorb the information. It is not enough to sit by and passively listen to a lecture or superficially engage in reading. Even if you are involved in a reading exercise it does not need to be passive. As you read, consider asking yourself questions or applying the information you are reading in some way.

The more sensory involvement you can engage in the faster you will learn. It is your responsibility to make sure that you are taking in the information in a way that will benefit you. As long as you are comfortable and relaxed in how you choose to take in the information, you will be able to absorb it more easily. There are several different approaches that can make that happen.

1. Look for the main idea first. Get a good overview of the project and try to understand it. The easiest way to do this is by looking at the chapter titles and subheadings first. Rather than read your text in

a chronological order, by first flipping through the subheadings and titles, you get the general idea of each lesson. Take the time to look at any images or illustrations that are there. This way, you have the basic idea down before you start to delve into the specifics.

2. Next you want to determine what is the main point of the lesson. This is key to getting a good understanding of what the purpose of the text is about. What is the point of the text, it's purpose, and how you can expect to benefit from it. Once you understand these elements, not only does the entire subject become more interesting, you are more likely to remember it for a longer period of time.

3. Take notes. Whether you will have the time or the desire later on to review them or not, the act of taking notes introduces another of your senses into the learning process. It adds the kinesthetic or bodily function to enhance and reinforce what you are learning.

1. Start by writing down everything you already know about the subject. This will help to boost your self confidence. You will begin to realize that you have some knowledge of the subject but it will also allow you to see exactly what areas you need to more knowledge in. By doing this you will be able to to zero in on your weak areas rather than use the session as a sporadic review of what you have already learned.

2. Take additional notes on areas you want to learn more about.

3. Create questions

4. Start an active search for the answers.

4. Divide the work into small bites. There is no doubt that tackling a huge textbook can be daunting, some of them can be hundreds of pages long. If it is a new topic or field of interest it can feel very intimidating. But if you take the time to divide the text up into smaller sessions, then you are less likely to be discouraged and end up giving up even before you get started. By breaking the material

up into smaller bite-sized study sessions, you can ensure that you will accomplish small successes without getting overwhelmed keeping your motivation and confidence in tact.

5. Ask questions. As you go through the lesson, continue to ask questions and then search for the answers. These are the facts and details that you will be most likely remember when needed. The act of asking questions is a means of keeping your mind focused on the topic. Of course there are many questions that could be asked about a subject but as a general rule, always make sure that you have the answers to the 5 Ws; who, what, when, where, and why. Who will tell you who's involved, what will identify its meaning and

purpose, when will give you a time frame, where will reveal the location, and why will answer its purpose. You could also ask the all-important How as well, which will tell you exactly how you can use the information and what affect it will have on your overall life in general.

Apply the Three Core Activities

Sometimes referred to as the VAK attack, this is when you apply the three most powerful elements of learning: Visual, Auditory, and Kinesthetic. This goes to the core of accelerated learning. We all absorb new information in completely different ways. These are the three primary ways we receive information. Learning through observation, hearing, and activities. While we all use all three ways to receive information, the majority of us have one that we prefer to rely on more. According to recent studies the percentages seem to be nearly equal when we are young with 29% preferring to receive information visually, 34% preferring auditory, and 37% with a strong preference towards kinesthetic.

However, studies also show that as we get older or preferences began to change with more people preferring visual learning over the other two. While we don't really know the reason behind this shift, some researchers point out that as much as 70% of our human body's sensory receptors are located in our eyes. In fact, in order for the retina of the eye to absorb light rays, it holds 120 million Rods and 7 million cones. Each of these rods and cones are designed to focus on a single tiny spec within our field of vision.

Keeping that thought in mind, studies performed at the University of Wisconsin have shown that when visual aids are used in learning, students experienced as much as 200% improvement in retention. Simply by adding visual aids to your study regimen will allow you to absorb the information must faster and easier.

To apply the VAK attack, you will have to approach the way you take in new information differently. You will have to start looking for things that are not explicitly spoken, listen for things that are not so blatantly heard, and feel things you've never felt before. You'll be looking under the surface for elements of the material that are not so easily seen.

While you may be able to absorb information in all three areas, it helps immensely when you know exactly which one of the three is your personal preference. That way, if you use study styles that incorporate your dominant sensory preference, you will capitalize on your strong suits and make your study time much more efficient.

Strategy #3 - Search Out the Meaning

We've said it before. In order for you to get the most out of a lesson or study session, it is important that you understand and can relate to it on a personal level. For this to happen, you need to focus on not just learning facts but on understanding the meaning of the lesson. When studying, the true meaning of a topic may not be readily seen and will require you to a) ask questions or b) look underneath the surface for more information.

To fully search out the meaning of something, it may be necessary to apply several different intelligences. Each one of us has at least nine possible ways to explore a topic in order to fully grasp the meaning behind any subject you choose to learn. By utilizing them in the right way you can fully create a learning style that takes advantage of your strengths and helps you to grow in knowledge.

By finding ways to use as many of these intelligences as possible it will trigger the mind to start thinking in totally different ways. A natural byproduct of this type of talent is that you will become more creative and innovative in your approach to many different things. Explore alternative options of study that go beyond the traditional school setting, which is primarily focused on logical and sequential presentation of a subject. However, when you engage in a topic that accesses all eight intelligences, you have a much better chance of hitting on one method that will be more efficient in teaching you the underlying meaning of a subject.

Finding Your Preferred Intelligence

Since we all have a unique collection of intelligences, you may find that you have more than one you rely on. Also, our battery of intelligence changes over the years. As we've already discussed, those who are younger get much more out of a kinesthetic and participatory form of study while those who are older prefer a more visual approach. Still, at any given time in your life, one and possible more forms will be your preferred method.

Linguistic: Those who are linguistically inclined enjoy playing word games, tongue-twisters, poetry, and stories. They are voracious readers willing to read everything in sight if given the opportunity. They are comfortable expressing themselves orally or in written form, and are very good storytellers. They usually have a strong vocabulary and are often asked to explain certain words they may use in conversation.

Logical-Mathematical: If you love working with numbers and can perform mathematical computations in your head, then you're probably strong in this area. People who are keenly interested in progressive advancements in science and enjoy experimenting with different things would also fall into this category. People who can balance their checkbook with ease, manage a budget, and enjoy extensively detailed vacations or business trips are also strong in logical mathematical intelligence. They enjoy brain teasers and puzzles and are quick to point out flaws in the logic of others around them.

Visual-Spatial: Those who appreciate the visual arts including paintings, sculpture, or drawing will be strong in this area of intelligence. They are excellent at keeping visual records of events by taking lots of pictures and videos. When idle, they enjoy doodling or taking notes on things they see around them. They can read a map easily and navigate the highways without problem. They are skilled at taking things apart just to see how they work.

Bodily-Kinesthetic: These are people who love sports and physical exercise. They enjoy taking walks, swimming, and the feeling they get after a really good workout. These are the type of people that need to physically handle something in order to understand it. They need the feel of the object between their fingers, to manipulate it, and maneuver it. They enjoy working on jigsaw puzzles or making things with their hands.

Musical: Those with musical intelligence are able to play some type of musical instrument, many are capable of singing - on key, and they are very adept at remembering a tune even if they have only heard it a few times. They prefer to listen to music wherever they are and enjoy attending musical events like concerts, plays, or symphonies. They have a good sense of rhythm and they find it difficult to imagine a life without some type of music as a big part of it. For them, music can easily trigger a wide range o emotions and visual imagery.

Interpersonal: These are people who enjoy working with others. They are excellent team players and enjoy being a part of a group or a committee. They make excellent mentors and advisors to others and because of that many seek them out for help in all sorts of problems. They prefer team activities like sports and games and are very social. They are excellent communicators and have no problem stepping up to the plate when something needs to be done.

Intrapersonal: These tend to be very introverted, preferring to spend more of their time with themselves. They enjoy solitude where they can reflect on the more important issues of life. They are independent and know their own mind. Many have their own hobbies or work that they prefer to do alone and enjoy sports like fishing and hiking, content with their own company. Intrapersonal people know themselves very well, clear on both their weaknesses and their strengths and prefer working for themselves rather than working for other people.

Naturalist: Those who are naturalists get the most enjoyment out of nature. They can easily recognize flora and fauna in their locale and have a keen interest in understanding how nature works in general. If given the opportunity, they can track wildlife, read the weather signs, and can visualize themselves in a natural climate. They love gardening, are concerned about the environment, and some have extended their interest in nature to the stars.

Existentialists: The newest of all the multiple intelligences is sometimes referred to as spiritual intelligence. These are people who are not afraid to examine the bigger and deeper meaning to life. They are highly sensitive to conceptualizing about the meaning of life and the purpose of our own human existence. They have a sense of cosmic wonder or a spiritual awareness that transcends much of what most people would consider in depth contemplation. These people tend to have what some might refer to as a sixth sense about the world around them, they are highly insightful, and some have even been described as having psychic abilities.

By applying each of your strong intelligences to your study, you literally become able to bring the information to life. It will become more memorable allowing you to interpret facts and examine them in their true nature. You can draw conclusions, do comparisons, and evaluate the importance of what you are learning and make it meaningful to you.

Keep in mind that your entire purpose for using these intelligences is to help you to not only absorb new knowledge but to find the meaning behind the information. This will give you a deeper understanding of what you are learning and find ways that can help you to relate to it on a more personal level.

Strategy #4 Activate Your Memory

The third step in the learning process is to activate your memory. You've probably already heard of those people who have what seems to be an infallible memory. They can recall details of events that may have happened years ago with amazing clarity. They have perfect recall.

After years of study of these people, scientists have been unable to uncover any distinguishable difference between the brains of these people and the brains of the average person. This leads us to believe that it is not *that* they have a unique mental ability but more a matter of *how* they use the same tools that we all have.

Activating your memory is merely a matter of applying several strategies that can help to lock the information into your long-term memory banks. There are three fundamental strategies that we have already talked about that will allow you to do this.

1. Put yourself in the right frame of mind before you begin studying
2. Find new ways to absorb the information that taps into your natural way of learning
3. Take the time to search out the deeper meaning of the information and apply it on a more personal level.

In all of those studies conducted on those with perfect recall, one thing did become very clear to researchers. Approximately 70% of new information you learn will be completely forgotten within a single 24-hour period if you do not take the necessary steps to store it in your long-term memory.

It is important to note that all people do not have the same ability to remember. Just like they have different strengths when it comes to intelligence, they also have different types of memories. Some people are better at remembering faces, others numbers, and others perhaps can remember names well. Very few people have the mastery over all aspects of memory. Still, everyone can improve their memory with the right strategies applied.

The key here is in *how* you introduce the new information into your mind. Our brain will automatically sift through information and does not pay much attention to the usual things. However, it will focus on those things that are unusual in nature. This is because our minds will automatically gravitate to those things that are odd, bizarre, funny, and even behaviors or conversations that fall outside of what is considered to be normal human conduct. So, you are more likely to remember that rude person in the supermarket than the polite cashier that you see every day.

The brain also naturally latches on to order. Even without realizing it, we group things together. Whether it is animals, scenes from nature, or simply your grocery list, even the most disorganized person has some level of mental order he needs to maintain. By organizing your material into categories, your brain will be more receptive to it because it engages you on an active level. You are creating associations between the different elements of the lesson and it will be easier to remember.

Making those associations is very important because your mind is like a vault used to store valuable knowledge. Think of all the millions of pieces of knowledge you have accumulated throughout your life. If there was no order to your mind, it would be literally impossible for you to retrieve any information when you needed it. With each passing day, you are accumulating and adding even more knowledge to your mind complicating the retrieval process even more.

But if you have an order to the information, language stored in one part of the brain, numbers in another, visual images in another, and in another place mathematical calculations and so on it will be much easier to find and retrieve the information you need. When there is an order to how to absorb your information, recalling it later will be much easier and definitely faster.

Of course, there are many different techniques you can use to trigger your memory so feel free to design your own memory aid. Remember your brain is unique and only you know exactly what works best for you. Just keep in mind that the key to triggering the memory is in how you acquire the information.

Once you believe you have successfully absorbed the information, give your brain time to register it and record it in its proper place. Often we forget things simply because we fail to perform this one step. Several studies have now shown that when you give your mind a rest, it allows the brain to actually file away any new information you've acquired into its proper place. This usually happens during the REM stage when you are sleeping, so make sure that you give your mind enough rest to ensure that you will recall it when you need it later on.

While this aspect of the brain is yet to be fully understood, research has shown that a simple three step process ensures that your new knowledge is firmly planted in the brain so that it can easily be recalled later.

1. Acquire the knowledge
2. Review the information just before going to sleep
3. Review the information again when you wake up

Strategy #5 Demonstrate Your New Knowledge

For years, parents have diligently asked their children the same question every day when they returned home from school. *What did you learn today?* The question seemed simple enough and for the parents it was simply a gauge to determine if their child was performing well in school. But now, as we come to understand how our brain works, we are realizing that this step has been very important in helping us to reinforce what we learned, literally locking in the lesson in our minds.

Demonstrating knowledge has powerful yet practical implications for anyone interested in accelerating their learning. It gives you the chance to apply your new knowledge in more meaningful ways and it helps you to see if you have any weak areas where you might have to work a little more to fill in the gaps.

If you have applied the first four strategies well, then you can consider this step a kind of test that will allow you to prove to yourself that you have truly learned the new material. To make sure that you really understand it and have the information locked in, you want to be able to recreate it in a different form.

Depending on what you have learned, there are a myriad different ways that you can demonstrate your new knowledge. Whatever you choose, make sure that you try to incorporate a variety of intelligences into the project. Some people prefer some of these suggestions:

- Review using flash cards
- Create a visual image of the new information
- Create tables, graphs, flow charts, etc.
- Make a list placing each element in order
- Repeat it back to themselves
- Explain it to someone else

Your choice of which technique to use will depend largely on your preferred learning style and the primary intelligences you utilize. Whatever method you choose, make sure that you look for errors in your conclusions, holes in your understanding, and weaknesses in your ability to demonstrate the knowledge. These are issues that should be addressed in your next study session.

Strategy # 6 Reflect on What You've Learned

Similar to the previous step, the final stage of accelerated learning is to take the time to reflect on what you have learned. This is the time to review and evaluate what new knowledge you have acquired and just how you plan to apply it in the future. This is when you take ownership of your new knowledge and find practical applications where you can.

One of the reasons people tend to forget so easily is because few rarely take the time to execute this step. However, self-analysis is the key to successful learning. While it may require taking the time to reflect on the material in a meaningful way, without this type of evaluation, your rewards will be limited.

It goes to understanding that your brain can only latch onto something if you're conscious of it. This point can't be emphasized enough. As a matter of fact, a research associate at the Harvard Graduate School of Education, David Perkins, has actively argued that there should actually be a tenth intelligence called "Reflective Intelligence" that we all must possess to some degree. He points out that not only do traditional schools fail to encourage this step in the learning process, those who do manage to develop the skill usually have to do so on their own.

Reflecting on a personal learning experience is important for everyone, regardless to whether they are in school or not. Reflection can be done in a variety of ways including writing in journals, creating charts, or in open discussions with others. When done well, it encourages the development of intrapersonal intelligence allowing the student to learn more about their own strengths and weaknesses.

If you're not accustomed to doing reflection exercises, it may be difficult at first but by asking some very basic questions, you can easily get your mind thinking in the right direction.

1. What went well
2. What could I have done better

3. How can I improve the next
   time

Once you learn to do an honest
appraisal of yourself then you'll be
able to fine tune your learning
sessions, literally tailoring them to
meet your unique and specific needs
no matter what you plan to study.

Chapter 5: How to Improve Your Memory and Why

There is a lot involved in learning how to learn. We've already discussed how understanding how your brain works and how your emotions impact your thought process when it comes to taking in new knowledge. However, we have only scratched the surface when it comes to true learning. Yes, all of the things we've discussed are of the utmost importance before you begin your course of study, but there is one more essential element that will be absolutely necessary in creating the right learning environment. That is your memory.

Without a good functioning memory, your ability to learn will only benefit you temporarily because as soon as you've stepped out of the learning environment, all your new knowledge will simply evaporate and will be of no lasting benefit to you. The fact is that you cannot bring your A Game to the table if you don't have any way of storing the new knowledge you acquire.

In order to get the most out of your study session, it will help immensely if you understand how your memory actually works, eventually that positive viewpoint will override these internal feelings and you will begin to believe them.

At this point, let's clarify what we're talking about here when we say memory. We're not talking about the mundane task of memorizing long lists of words, facts, or phrases that are often assigned in traditional classroom settings. Memory in this context is your ability to store information in your brain in a way that makes it easy to retrieve when you need it in the future. There are three basic steps to creating a memory:

1. Encoding
2. Storage
3. Retrieval

If any one of these steps is not executed properly, the information you achieve could be lost somewhere in your brain only to reappear at the wrong time. When you cannot retrieve it when needed, then the whole process of learning becomes moot.

Encoding: As you learn information, your brain needs to process all of the data that it receives from your senses. You may not be aware of it but your brain is constantly at work sifting through all of the information and coding it either in your conscious or your subconscious mind. This is a very important fact to help you to remember details better.

There are several factors that determine exactly if and where your brain will store all your information.

1. The amount of attention you giving this new information
2. Your motivation or desire to know it
3. Your emotional and psychological state
4. The number of distractions....

If you are devoted to the lesson and giving it the needed attention then your brain will work harder to store the information in a place where you can access it later. However, if you are distracted, watching a movie at the same time, or otherwise uninterested in the topic, the brain may store the information in your short-term memory banks. But it will require a special combination of requirements to be met for that data to pass through the gate and find its way to your long-term memory, the most treasured place in the mind.

Storage: After the information is encoded, the brain then must decide where it will be go. Think of it like a massive file cabinet and the new information is a file that needs to be put away. There are three different types of memory storage systems you need to know about.

1. Sensory
2. Short-term
3. Long-term

Sensory memory is the shortest of the three. These thoughts are stored just long enough so they can be transferred to your short-term memory if needed. It allows information collected by your five senses to be held in place for a short time after the original stimulus is no longer present. A good example of sensory memory is when you get a glimpse of something before it completely disappears from view. For a few moments after the view of it has faded, the brain will continue to hold its impression for.. There are two primary forms of sensory memory, iconic or visual memory and echoic or audio memory.

Retrieval: the final step of creating a memory is the retrieval phase, which is what we are often referring to when we recall something to mind. The brain retrieves stored memories in different ways. There are some things you will be able to remember without any specific trigger and there are other memories that will require a cue to bring them up. Other memories may only be recalled in a particular sequence or as a part of a group (think of your favorite song collection) you probably recall those songs in a very specific order; your ABCs, or reciting a poem. Usually, the way this type of memory is stored is determined by just how much attention you gave to the learning process. As you can probably gather, few things actually have the honor of reaching your retrieval memory. To reach this point, the memory must be encoded deeply and have formed many connections over time.

Understanding these basic functions of how the memory works helps us to see why cramming for an exam is not an effective learning technique. When you spend long hours studying just before an exam, you are storing what you've learned in your short-term memory because you know it must remain there for at least a day or more. However, your level of attention begins to wane after a time because you don't really have a commitment to recall the information after you have completed the test. This means your motivation is not very strong so the brain will store the information in a space that exists somewhere between your long-term and your short-term memories. In other words, it won't be encoded deeply into your long-term memory and without reinforcement, it will begin to fade.

To accelerate your learning, you goal is to improve your memory capacity and train your brain to create deeper connections that will lock in your new knowledge for longer periods of time.

Forgetfulness

We all forget things from time to time. It is part of the human process However, when you are trying to improve your ability to learn you also need to focus on how to strengthen your memory so you don't lose what you are working so hard to learn. To do this, we really need to take a little time to figure out exactly why we forget things.

In truth, forgetfulness is simply a weakness in the brain's ability to store or to retrieve information. For example, if information is misfiled in the short-term memory banks rather than the long-term chances are if you need to recall it six-months later, it won't be available for retrieval. Your inability to find it is actually a problem with how deeply the information has been embedded.

There are three ways the brain will try to retrieve the information stored within it.

1. Recall
2. Recognition
3. Relearning

When you recall something you are remembering it without any prompting or cue. We do this when we recite lists of things without any external aids. We recall our ABCs, our home address, phone numbers, and our birthdays. These are so strongly embedded into our minds that we have no fear of forgetting them no matter what may happen. Most people can remember their first home address even though they have not lived there for decades. It's because it has been rehearsed repeatedly or you have placed a lot of importance to retaining this knowledge that the brain gives it considerably more attention than anything else.

Recall is the strongest form of memory you can have so it is also the most difficult to achieve. For something to be stored in your recall, you will usually have to dedicate many hours of practice or study to get it there yet, this is the area that we are targeting when we are trying to achieve accelerated learning.

Recognition is the type of memory that requires a cue to bring it to mind. We often do this type of memory when we hear one or two notes from a song. As soon as you hear those notes, your mind will immediately bring up the entire song in an instant but without that cue, it is almost impossible to remember. You also use recognition when you need to remember different associated facts. For example, you may not be able to remember all the countries of the world and their capitals but if you were given a clue, a rhyme or a song, it would be much easier for you to bring them to mind.

To use this to your advantage, try to create an unusual mental picture of your lesson so that your brain will latch onto it and you'll have a much better chance of recalling the information to mind when you need it. For this type of memory, mnemonics, and other similar study tools tend to work best. Since we may have a limited amount of time to dedicate to study, we naturally use these devices to group the new data together into recognizable chunks and rely on the cues to help us to remember them.

Finally, relearning - the weakest form of memory, occurs during the review process of study. It is a systematic approach where you use less and less effort to study it each time you access this type of information. For example, you may receive a specific list of information at work on Monday. The first day you receive the data, it may take you 30 minutes to get through it all but the next day, it may only require you to spend half that time. By the end of the week, you will probably get through it with a cursory glance.

However, if the data is only good for a single week, the following week you won't recall it because you haven't committed it to your long-term memory yet. This often happens when you learn a new language in school. You may be required to learn 20, 30 or more words every day and you will do well absorbing the information. By reviewing the information on a regular basis you may feel that you have mastered the topic. However, once class is over and you are no longer using that information, it will fade surprisingly quickly. This is where the expression "use it or lose it" comes from. When you store information in this stage, you have not yet taken the steps to put the information into your long-term memory banks so in time, no matter how good you may be at it, it will begin to fade.

So, it is easy to see that learning is not just about our ability to absorb new information but the key to its success is on enhancing our memory and making sure that what we absorb is encoded and stored properly for easy retrieval. Our brain's have a natural disposition to get rid of information as soon as it can, so we have to be ever diligent on how we store it from the very beginning.

We all have something called a "forgetting curve" where our brains slowly begin to sift out information after we have learned it. In essence, our memories begin to decay after a surprisingly short period of time if you do not take some action to reinforce it. For example, if you read a new lesson one day it may seem to have made a very strong impression on your mind, however, within just a few days, you're probably wondering what you really took in or if you've learned anything at all. Chances are, you will probably remember only half of it after as little as four days and in about a week, your memory will drop to around 30%.

The point here is that without review, in time, what you have learned will disappear to practically nothing. However, with regular review and practice, you can easily push your memory back closer to the 100% mark with just a little investment in time.

From just understanding how the brain sifts through information, discarding things that it does not perceive as valuable, it can help you to maximize the benefits you might receive from your study sessions. As you begin to learn about your forgetting curve, your goal with each study period is to reduce its decline, attempting to lower your percentages as much as possible by reducing the amount of memory decay you can naturally expect after each learning session.

To do this, we need to understand this type of decline better. According to some research studies, the rate of decline could be reduced if several factors are in place. First, this rate could significantly be reduced if the memory being stored was proven to have some level of personal significance and second, the age of the memory played a major role in how quickly we began to remember.

This informs us that there is little we can do to reduce the impact of information loss due to the forgetting curve, but it does suggest that there are things we can do to ensure that the information is stored in the proper area of our brains to make sure that it is easier to bring to mind when it is needed.

Our ability to remember information is our primary goal but we should expect more. As we have begun to realize, we should be continuously aiming for what we learn to reach recall memory above all else and recognition as our fallback goal. So, the question should now be, how to use this information to make us better and more efficient learners. The answer is simple, *retrieval practice.*

In the traditional sense, we consider learning to be a method where we absorb new information in our brains. A purely passive act, there is little of what we do invested into the learning process. However, now that we understand how memory works, we can see why this is only half of the learning process. When we learn something passively, we may come to understand it at the time but unless we personally invest in the study process, making study more of an activity, we are not likely to be able to retrieve that information later on when we need it.

This is where retrieval practice can be of help. Rather than getting into a continuous practice of accumulating more knowledge, we can stop periodically and pull information out of our brains instead. By making practical application of the knowledge we have already absorbed, we reinforce the memories we've already stored making them much easier to recall over time.

We can do this by using prompts to help us to put the memory to good use. One of the most common and familiar methods of retrieval practice is the use of flash cards. The front of the card is the cue and the back of the card is the information we've already learned.

This is one of the best ways to boost your memory, especially when dealing with facts. Once you understand how it works, you'll see why this simple method of memory training is so effective.

First off, retrieval practice is an active skill. In your brain, it demands that you process the image or clue through thinking and searching out the data until you finally are able to retrieve the information you need. Repeated practice in this way will eventually move the memory from the recognition type of memory to recall where you will learn this information without the need of any clues to help you get to it.

How to Make Good Use of Retrieval Practice

One of the main reasons why retrieval practice has proven to be so effective is because it requires you to take an active role in the learning process. Rather than simply trying to absorb information that others give you, it is necessary for you to invest in actually doing something to reinforce the learning.

Now that we understand how our memories are stored and activated, we realize that retrieval practice is simply a means of making it easier for you to remember new things and "retrieve" these new concepts from the stores in our brain. So, in essence, learning should be more than just putting information in, it should also involve strategies that help you to pull it out when needed.

While flashcards are an excellent example of retrieval practice, we do not have to limit ourselves with these. In fact, they are not the actual strategy but merely a tool that allows us to apply the strategy in one form of retrieval practice. Actually, most people do not use flashcards to their best advantage and so do not really reinforce their learning in the right way.

For example, many use flashcards with a more passive approach. They see the cue, answer the card, flip it over to check their answer and move on to the next card. This may appear to be the obvious use but if if you change just one single element you can boost your memory even more. Simply by taking the added step of saying the answer **out loud** suddenly turns this into a more active form of study. This may seem like a pretty small difference but an essential one just the same. The act of vocalizing the answer before moving on actually engages more of your senses and involves more brain activity for the information to process.

Of course, in real life, there may not be any flashcards to rely on, there may not be a teacher around to give you the needed cues, and you may not have any additional external assistance to help you to retrieve the information you need. However, that does not mean that retrieval practice is not possible. We can still use flashcards as an example only using the basic methodology in more complex strategies.

Whether you're studying information for school or for work, you can create your own flashcards but instead of placing verbal cues or equations on the cards, try using concepts on the front and explanations on the back. Remember, earlier in the book we talked about learning concepts before facts. So, once you understand the concepts create flashcards for them following these basic rules:

- Reword the concepts in simple English
- Write a plot or an example that demonstrates the concept
- Apply the concept to a real-life experience
- Write the opposite of the concept

- Draw a visual image of the concept

So, rather than your flashcards written literally, you can write them so that they cover more abstract matters of the lesson. By using this approach, you actually push your brain to think beyond the written word and be able to extract more detailed information that may not actually be included in the lesson itself.

Once you've mastered those, then you can create another set of flashcards that deal with the minute details surrounding your particular concept. Placing all of the flashcards within the context of a concept will help you to gain a deeper understanding of them and find more immediate applications in real life.

Chapter 6: What Mistakes Really Mean

Learning can be either passive or active depending on how much you are willing to invest in it. You could think of it as if you are looking at the past and extracting concepts that may at first seem insignificant to you and sifting through them, searching out what they could really mean to your life and storing in a safe place until needed. There is no end to the different types of learning techniques you can use to help you to do this so it is very tempting to try all sorts of new and exciting ideas as you hear from them.

Unfortunately, many of those learning strategies could prove to be very ineffective and time consuming when you're trying to absorb that information at an accelerated rate. You can avoid this by learning how to identify these time wasters before you begin and creating your own methods for correcting them. This will help you to avoid making unnecessary mistakes that could lead to slowing down your learning process.

Have the Right Mindset

Again, it is important to consider your personal attitude towards learning. According to Dr. Carol Dweck of Stanford University, most people have either one of two primary mindsets in their approach to study.

Those with a **fixed** mindset hold to the belief that certain traits as intelligence and talent are inborn and genetic. Therefore, these things are something you either have or you don't and there is very little that can be done to change that. Those with this mindset usually do not do well in studies because they feel that their efforts will not yield results unless they are part of the select few that are born with the needed qualities to master the skills they are trying to achieve.

These are the people that will limit their studies so they only concentrate on areas where they are confident that they will succeed and take steps to avoid anything that may require them to struggle or create a possibility that they will fail. This allows them to avoid criticism, or to have to show any sign of weakness or flaws in their body of knowledge.

Those with a **growth** mindset however, are more willing to take on more challenging work. They feel that they can master any topic that holds their interest if they have enough tenacity and put in enough effort to do so. They are persistent enough to push through barriers, possible limitations, and aren't afraid of critical feedback from others but will use that information as inspiration to spur them onto more learning opportunities.

Your viewpoint in this regard will determine how you will view the challenges and setbacks that you receive. If you have a fixed mindset then likely you will conclude that your ability to learn that particular subject or skill is not within you reach. So, when you make a mistake, you will subconsciously view it as fate and there is little you can do about it. If on the other hand, you have a growth mindset, then you may view those same mistakes as a means to expand your skills, use them as stepping stones to your ultimate goal. It is clear from just this single point what type of view works best with the accreted learning method.

The results of several research studies emphasized this very point. Of the subjects studied, those with a fixed mindset focused more on the type of results that gave them a better chance at success while those with a growth mindset looked for opportunities that would allow them to expand their abilities. In essence, their view of success was different. One group saw learning something new as success while the other group viewed success as avoiding mistakes.

In addition, those with the fixed mindset found they were only interested in getting data that showed their present abilities with no expectations of change in the future whereas those with a growth mindset showed zero interest in getting the right answer but were instead concerned with any information that would allow them to grow in their knowledge and develop new skills and talents. They saw no negative aspect to getting the wrong answer but were interested in any information that will allow them to advance their personal development.

In short, those with the growth mindset were focused on learning while those with the fixed mindset were more focused on avoiding mistakes.

This type of mental development occurs when we are very young and if not adjusted later on will remain with us throughout our entire lifetime. The good news is that even though we may have a fixed mindset, it is not a permanent viewpoint but can be changed. Just like any other mental habit, we can learn to mentally switch to a growth mindset, thus making it possible for us to make sure that we continue to expand our knowledge every time we set out to learn something new.

We can change our viewpoint simply by applying intervention techniques. With very small, sometimes minuscule adjustments we can gradually begin to change the way we view learning in general.

One way to do this is with praise. When you compliment someone who has made a mistake you open up their minds just a tiny bit to allow a more positive viewpoint to start to take shape. Of course, you don't want to compliment the mistake itself, but you can always find something positive to say to someone. For example, you might see a mistake but compliment them on their approach to the answer like: "I can really see that you struggled with this problem but I admire the fact that you didn't quit. You now turn their focus to the process of learning the correct method without blatantly criticizing the specific mistake.

When you praise someone based on their skills or abilities, you are reinforcing the idea that the skill needed is not an inborn trait that cannot be changed. This is sort of like complimenting someone based on their genetic physical appearance. You are giving them credit for something they had no control over. However, praise the effort; how she did her hair, applied make up, or the selection of clothes, you are now looking at the effort they have put into enhancing their appearance. The action they they have taken. The goal is to compliment the effort not the genetics.

The more you praise the effort, the easier it will be for the person to be motivated to put in more effort in the future. This can be a practice you apply in everyday life, in all your interactions with other people. By making this a practice, you make it easier for others to accept constructive criticism, and build up the anticipation of learning new things in the future. By extension, by your practicing this type of praise and freely offering it to others, you also reinforce those same ideas into your own mind. You'll learn just how to evaluate your own behavior when you are faced with learning something completely new.

Another Way to View Mistakes

Often mistakes are not a result of a lack of effort on the part of the student. They could be a direct result of how the information was received during the lesson. We've already discussed how our minds are geared towards certain learning styles. Once we know what our primary form of intelligence is, it is easy to expect that if information is taught in that vein it will be much easier for us to absorb. However, we may not always have the luxury of receiving information in our preferred format. This does not mean that we can't learn but it may indicate that we will have to work a little harder to absorb the new information and in the process, we will make mistakes.

There are actually some biological factors that give support to this theory. Our multiple intelligences are not purely by accident. The structures of our brains are what actually make us strong in one area or another. Consider these biological facts:

Visual: Occipital lobes control the visual sense. The occipital and parietal lobes are key in controlling spatial orientation.

Aural: The temporal lobes are responsible for all your auditory content and the right temporal lobe is primarily used for music.

Verbal: Controlled by the temporal and frontal lobes primarily located in the Broca's and Wernicke's regions of the brain.

Physical: The cerebellum and the motor cortex located at the very back of the frontal lobe controls the majority of our physical movement.

Logical: Controlled primarily by the parietal lobe on the left side of the brain. The area that focuses on our ability to think logically.

Social: The frontal and temporal lobes are responsible for how we manage social activities. Our limbic system also has an influence on what we do in a social environment as well as what we do when we are alone. It controls our emotions and our moods.

Intrapersonal: Controlled mostly by the frontal and parietal lobes and our limbic system.

Even with these scientific facts before us, there is nothing to say that our brains are so fixed that we can't learn in different ways. For example, if a person were to lose his sights in an accident, losing his visual intelligence will not stop him from learning. He will however, need to build up his abilities in the other senses and eventually will be able to continue to learn. This is evidence that shows that even though we have a preferred form of intelligence, we have within us to ability to adapt and use other intelligences when needed.

The idea of multiple intelligences has met with a certain level of resistance due to the fact that some have concluded that you can't learn unless you acquire information in your preferred learning style. However, while it may be your preferred learning style, it is not your only learning style. In reality, you can learn in different styles as long as you are willing to adjust your level of focus and commitment to the study.

By concluding that you can only learn with one predominant style you are limiting yourself, which can only work to your disadvantage. It is true that based on these natural intelligences, you may gravitate more towards one style than another however, by reinforcing your learning through use of several different styles of learning you not only increase your chances of building up knowledge but you engage more of your brain activity in the entire process.

Remember, learning happens much faster when you are an active participant. You learn even better when you are motivated. So, find ways to become more active in the process from start to finish. This could mean taking notes, making it more meaningful to you, explaining it to others, etc. All of this could lead to errors in your conclusions however, you can choose to view those errors as a blight on your abilities or you can use them as stepping stones to better understanding.

Nearly all learning in life is based on the trial and error method. Making a mistake is not a reflection on your personal character or even on your ability to master a certain skill. You can choose to allow it to derail your learning process and discourage you or you can view that mistake as a way to practice new knowledge, a chance to find better solutions to the problem you already have and opening yourself up to grow in your knowledge.

Chapter 7: What Mistakes Really Mean

Once you have mastered your new knowledge or new skill, the learning process is not yet complete. If you are properly motivated, there is a good chance that you will want to do more than just learn this new topic, you'll also want to build on it and become expert in your field. To do this, it will become necessary for you to reinforce what you have already learned. There are numerous strategies that will help you to cement your new knowledge into your brain, some you will find will work well for you and others will not. Choose the ones that will work best for you or use the ideas generated here to create some methods that are more suited to your personal learning style.

10,000 Hours

While learning the basics of anything can be mastered in a few sessions, to become proficient in that same subject requires that you have to at some point stop learning and start doing. You can learn the fundamentals of anything from a book but if you ever hope to claim your experience in the skill or talent, you will at some point have to close that book and put what you've learned into practice.

Think about all the things that you learned in your life; riding a bicycle, swimming, dancing, or even just mastering the ability to read. While you may have understood the principles behind what you read, a time came when it was necessary to reinforce that knowledge with actual practice.

According to a research project designated to studying proficient violin players in Berlin, of those players that were most proficient, they averaged approximately 10,000 hours of practice over the course of building up their talent. Those that ranked on the average level only reported approximately 4,000 hours each.

This information helps us to see that in order to become "expert" in skill at any endeavor we might want to undertake, we need to stop studying and start practicing. Over the years, we have seen firsthand the benefits of extensive practice. While we may view these people as overnight successes, before these people were viewed as "experts" in their field by others, they had amassed countless hours of diligent practice and work to reach that point.

This type of rule can apply to just about anything we decide we want to learn. Few people take on a study project only to get a basic understanding of it but in fact, want to reach a point where they can excel in the subject. You can apply this to anything from cooking to zoology, the more time you set aside to practice what you have learned the stronger you entrench those teachings into your mind.

Learning is one thing, mastery is something else entirely. In order to become proficient in anything, you must be willing to invest both time and patience in your subject. This book is about accelerated learning not about becoming efficient in any prospect. So, as you begin to learn about different things, you will have to tailor your expectations so that you don't expect too much too fast. If you apply the techniques found in this book, you will learn at a faster pace but to develop an expert status, there is only one way to get there, with a regular commitment of time and realistic expectations.

Still, practice has to be done in a very specific way. If you are just working on something by rote, then your mind is not fully committed to it. Repetitious exercises will help you to develop muscle memory but will only allow you to establish a system of consistent movements throughout, making the more automatic. This type of practice does nothing to boost your level of intelligence.

Deliberate practice though, requires you to put more mental effort into the task, breaking it down into smaller and smaller parts, repeating them over and over again, taking mental note of the areas where you need to focus more attention on improvement. Deliberate practice is far more involved than just practicing by rote. While it involves mastering the things you understand, it also involves finding those weak areas and taking the initiative to find the information to fill in the gaps, rounding out your knowledge so that it is a complete package. It involves several steps.

- Identifying your needs
- Examining your weaknesses
- Finding possible solutions
- Testing your theories
- Getting feedback
- Refocusing your efforts

Continuing with these steps until you reach your overall goal helps you to practice in a way that will allow you to build your expertise and thus reinforce your knowledge in a way that you can grow from.

You must be careful though. There is the risk of slipping into mundane rote work if you can't keep your mind focused properly. You also need to give extra attention that you are in fact, reinforcing your knowledge in the wrong way. If you've learned the information correctly then everything will work well but if you didn't acquire the information correctly, you could end up simply reinforcing bad habits and not improving at all. This is why, it is often a good idea to get external feedback from experts to make sure you're on the right track.

Your goal should be not just to learn new knowledge but to learn it in such a way that you can apply it accurately. That way you will be able to identify the mistakes and find new ways to solve them correctly.

However, the results of newer research also tells us that in order to reinforce what we have learned, we need to do more than just practice it. Intensive practice has proved beneficial in certain areas like sports, music, games, and the arts but other areas weren't able to show such a significant increase, indicating that some professional goals you may have for yourself may need more than just practice to make sure that you find success.

The 80/20 Rule

The 80/20 rule is a common rule that simply states that within any given set of circumstances; only 20% of the components are considered to be important while the other 80% are trivial. This is an important reminder that everything we absorb through the learning process is not essential information that will help us to grow.

We see this in normal brain biology. Our brains are natural filters that sift out much of the data our senses collect every day. It carefully selects what information is important and should be remembered while your glimpse of the hummingbird you saw six months ago while you were watering your garden is not essential to what you need stored in your long-term memory.

As you study, it is important that you learn how to identify what that 20% of important information is. This can be applied in just about every avenue of life. Notice these facts:

- 80% of sales comes from 20% of customers
- 80% of company tasks are performed by 20% of the employees
- 80% of happy people are found in only 20% of relationships

- 80% of travels can be highlighted in only 20% of the experiences

These points only serve to reinforce the fact that all knowledge contains the ability to help you grow. You become expert in any area by making sure you're not wasting a lot of time on trivial points but can determine what points of the lesson are the most important.

This does not mean that you need to ignore everything else but the additional information should be considered as supplementary and does not need to take up the lion's share of your attention during the study time. Attack the important elements first and then once those are mastered, go back and address the supplemental information later.

Teaching Others

Probably, the most rewarding method for reinforcing your newfound knowledge is teaching it to someone else. When you are required to take your subject and break it down and explain it to others it not only cements the knowledge in your own mind but it also helps you to better identify the flaws in your own thinking.

By teaching others, you are able to see both sides of the learning process, which can give you valuable insight into how others absorb the same information. Their questions can prove to be very insightful in highlighting areas of the topic you may not have considered. It is probably the most active of all learning styles. Remember that the more engaged you are in the process the better you'll be able to master it. Consider these estimates:

- You remember 90% of what you learn if you teach others or use your new knowledge immediately
- You remember 75% when you practice what you learn
- You remember 50% when you participate in group discussions
- 30% when you observe a demonstration
- 20% if you watch an audio-visual presentation
- 10% if you read it
- 5% if you listen only

These are mere estimates of what retention is but it does go to show that the more involved you are in the process the better your ability to learn.

There is no question that teaching is about as active as it can get. It not only cements the information in your mind but it forces you to look at the matter from different angles, exposing gaps in your understanding and sending you back to the basics to find the answers you need. It's a way of testing your knowledge and proving to yourself if you know it or not.

Chapter 8: Preparing to Learn for Life

Learning is a lifelong experience that doesn't stop when you finish school. Our brains have been uniquely designed so that it is in constant search of new information so we all need to rethink the common viewpoint that says that we should stop learning at a certain point. In fact, a significant part of life's experiences stem from our learning. We marvel at the wonders of the universe, technology is constantly advancing, and knowledge in today's modern age is growing exponentially year after year. We need to be consistent learners just to keep up with the constant changes in our every day life. In order to be successful in this type of endeavor, we need to view learning as a life habit rather than just a phase we go through.

Habits are activities we do so much that they become a part of our subconscious behavior. We do these things automatically, without thought, in much the same way as we might view chewing our food when we eat. Becoming an accelerated learner may not be easy at first. We may have to practice these techniques repeatedly until we reach a point where we can slip into learning mode and are able to make it a natural part of our lives.

When learning becomes a habit, it's a clear indication that we have mastered the skill so well that we don't need to give it extra thought. It then becomes part of our recall memory. But how do you develop your learning skills to that point? There are several things you must keep in mind.

Be Persistent

Your ability to remain focused on your lessons and follow through even when things are tough will help you to develop good learning habits. When you consistently work to create new strategies to tackle those big problems and refuse to let them discourage you, eventually, you'll reach a point where learning will become second nature to you. However, in order to accomplish this, you will have to become comfortable with dealing with things that may not be very clear, to be okay when things are not laid out plainly in black and white. You'll also need to develop some flexibility in your study plan. Give yourself some options so you're not falling into a rut of repeating the same things over and over again. This way, you'll be more likely to have an open mind when tackling new problems and challenges as they present themselves.

Another element of persistence is patience. This may not be a problem when the learning is easy and information is readily understood, but frustration tends to step in when you are faced with problems that are difficult to understand. It's coming to grips with the idea that you will meet with obstacles that may restrict your comprehension, that you will make mistakes, and you will face challenges. If you are persistent, you won't allow these factors to disrupt your learning but will use them skillfully in forging ahead until you reach the point of mastery.

It will require a certain level of self-discipline so you can remain focused and approach your learning in a deliberate manner. The impulse may be to throw it all aside for something easy, but resisting that urge and pushing through will be the key to your success. Learning to think before giving into impulse reactions will help you to accomplish what you set out to do and will keep you on the path to accelerated learning.

Be Flexible

A good learner will be flexible enough to adapt their techniques to the problems before them. Mental flexibility will allow you to develop an open mind so that you can shift your thinking when you reach a point where you face an obstacle. Rather than allowing that to block your growth, if you are flexible enough, you will find ways around the problem and approach it from a completely different angle if need be.

Flexibility also means overcoming preconceived ideas about what you believe to be true. This is much easier to do if you enter the learning process with positive emotions rather than allowing negative feelings to come into play. Remember, you're looking for a long-term solution to a problem and not some type of quick fix. While you may have previously believed that the solution to a problem is one way, leave yourself open to alternatives that you may uncover during your studies that could make the process easier.

Reach for Quality, not Quantity

When you are studying with the aim of being accurate, your time will produce quality results. It's not how much you study it is how much you get from your study. When your focus is on acquiring the right information rather than how much information, you are less likely to make mistakes in your hurry to the finish line; you'll pay more attention to detail, check, and then double check your results so you can be sure that the finished product of your efforts will yield reliable results that you can use going forward.

Because of this, you'll be less likely to take shortcuts but take your study seriously. While you can ask others for help, try to only get them to give you options and don't rely on them to do the heavy lifting for you. This is your learning experience and the more you trust yourself to work out the problems the more benefit you will receive from it.

To become a lifelong learner, means that you will have to not just approach a learning session as a one-time event but see every lesson you undertake as a major part of your life. Learning should not be viewed as something you do in addition to your normal routine but it should be a part of who you are as a person. Learn to love to learn and when you do, you will be able to develop the kind of habits that will provide you with all you need to continue to grow in knowledge and wisdom until the very end of your days.

Conclusion

Thank you again for downloading this book!

I hope this book was able to help you to be able to develop those skills that will help you to benefit from being a lifelong learner.

In this book we have discussed a lot of information that will not only make you a better student but will help you to develop the habits that have earmarked people for success for generations. We have learned:

- How your mental state of mind can impact how you learn

- How your brain receives and processes information

- How to M.A.S.T.E.R learning by following the six-step plan to accelerate your learning

- How to prepare your mind so it is more receptive to learning

- How to boost your memory so that you can access your wealth of new knowledge

- And how to reinforce all that new knowledge so that it is less likely to fade over time

Learning is not something that we do simply as a means to get by. In today's modern age, knowledge is growing at an impressively rapid rate making it necessary for all of us, young and old, to be on a continuous learning cycle. Never before in our human history has so much information been so easily accessible, and it is changing constantly.

This means that we have to be ever vigilant in keeping our minds open to new shifts in how our world works. The only way to successfully navigate such rapid moving waters is to accelerate your learning so that you can grow right along with the rest of the world. By applying these simple basic strategies contained here in this book, you will not only be able to keep up with the rapid flow of information coming your way, you'll be able to enjoy it to.

The next step is to take this information to heart and put it into practice.

Finally, if you enjoyed this book, then I'd like to ask you for a favor, would you be kind enough to leave a review for this book on Amazon? It'd be greatly appreciated!

Thank you and good luck!

31493429R00102

Made in the USA
Middletown, DE
02 January 2019